99 Strategies for Making Your Marriage Last Forever

How to Give and Get the Very Best in Your Marriage

DR. DWAYNE L. BUCKINGHAM

RHCS

An Imprint of RHCS Publishing

Also by Dr. Dwayne L. Buckingham

Unconditional Love, Marriage Edition

Unconditional Love, Marriage Edition (Workbook)

You Deserve More, A Single Woman's Guide to Marriage:
How to Select and Invest in a Lifetime Partner

Resilient Thinking: The Power of Embracing Realistic and
Optimistic Thoughts about Life, Love and Relationships

The Empathic Leader: An Effective Management Model for
Enhancing Morale and Increasing Workplace Productivity

Qualified, yet Single: Why Good Men Remain Single

Can Black Women Achieve Marital Satisfaction: How
Childhood Nurturing Experiences Impact Marital Happiness

Unconditional Love: What Every Woman and Man Desires
in a Relationship

A Black Woman's Worth: My Queen and Backbone

A Black Man's Worth: Conqueror and Head of Household

www.realhorizonsdlb.com

99 Strategies for Making Your Marriage Last Forever

Additional copies of this book can be purchased on-line at www.realhorizonsdlb.com or by contacting:

R.E.A.L. Horizons Consulting Service, LLC
P.O. Box 2665
Silver Spring, MD 20915
240-242-4087 Voice mail

Expanding Horizons by keeping it "R.E.A.L."

FIRST EDITION

Cover designed by RHCS Publishing

Library of Congress Control Number: 2015938017

ISBN: 978-0-9855765-8-5

Edited by Laren Westy and Sharon Taylor

For Worldwide Distribution

Printed in the United States of America

Dedication

To every man and woman who desires to give and get the very best in his or her marriage and make it last forever.

Table of Contents

Introduction

Marriage is a lifetime commitment and those of us who agree to share the remainder of our lives with our chosen loved one, do so with the hope that our marriage will last forever. We enter marriage with an optimistic view about our relationship and spouse.

Thoughts of being with our spouse forever run rampantly through our minds daily. "I am so in love with you" is said with enthusiasm. No wrongs are worth arguing over in the beginning stage of marriage. Difficult-to-cope-with qualities such as stubbornness and inflexibility are minimized or are addressed in a positive and patient manner. Personality and value differences are viewed as strengths instead of obstacles. We believe in and preach, "Where I am weak, you are strong."

Love rules our marriage and feelings of inseparability are enough to persuade both individuals to support each other through the good and bad. We soar off of love in the beginning and are willing to do whatever it takes to make our marriage last forever. However, after the exhilarating feeling of being in love declines, reality sets in (children, career shifts, finances, etc.), and unfortunately the dynamics of our marriage change.

Difficult-to-cope-with qualities such as stubbornness and inflexibility are now seen as such, and are typically addressed in a negative or belittling manner. Personality and value differences are viewed as obstacles instead of strengths. Some of us state, "We are so different and this is why we have so many problems in our marriage." Striving to make your marriage last forever becomes exhausting and leads some of us to question why we got married in the first place. Depending on the intensity and number of stressors in the marriage, one or both individuals might say, "I love you, but I am not in love with you anymore." Love is still present, but is slowly fading.

Does any of this sound familiar?

I pray to God that I am not the only one who has experienced some of this in my marriage. However, if I am, I am glad to report that my discouragement and frustration did not last long.

One day while sitting on the couch (feeling hopeless) in my man cave (basement) listening to an old school R&B mixed album, I was inspired. As I sat, song after song played and I listened hopelessly. Then, "Make It Last Forever" by Keith Sweat came on. As I listened to the song I felt like Keith Sweat was talking to me personally. Keith sung out, "Got to make it, got to make it, got to make (Ho...oh...), got to make it, oh, baby."

After listening to "Make It Last Forever," I felt inspired and realized that it was my responsibility, as head of my household, to try to make my love and marriage last forever. As the lyrics of the song resonated in my soul, I asked myself the following questions: "Can I live happily ever after? Is it possible to make my marriage last forever?

Like me, you have probably asked yourself similar questions and I am here to tell you that the answer to both questions is a resounding "Yes!"

Let me clarify: the answer is "Yes": if, and only if, you are willing to do some work. I got off the couch and invested a significant amount of time nurturing my love for my wife and our marriage. Now, I see marriage for what it is: a God-ordained relationship that is filed with an array of emotions and thoughts that must be understood and addressed on a regular basis, especially as life shifts and the relationship evolves.

I realized that there is no such thing as a perfect marriage because God did not create perfect people. This realization is what makes marriage last forever. Marital bliss and longevity is a by-product of work, which requires effort, time and energy. Experiencing ups and downs is part of the marital journey, but divorce should never be an option.

What you will find in this marriage revival book is a list of 99 Marriage Sustainment Strategies that I have compiled from my work with thousands of married couples who have experienced marital bliss for 20 years or more. As an experienced psychotherapist with more than seventeen years of experience in providing marital therapy, I have personally witnessed the happiness of couples who have successfully applied the strategies outlined in this book. If these strategies are applied consistently and sincerely, you too can experience the love that you felt in the beginning of your marriage and be on the road toward making your marriage last forever.

As you read this book, be mindful that your success will be determined by the quality of work that you do. Remember that "Make" is an action word, which means you have to do something. To make your marriage last forever you must make time to be proactive, patient, positive, pleasant and passionate. By doing all of these things and applying the 99 Marriage Sustainment Strategies in this book, you will be empowered to give and get the very best in your marriage and make it last forever.

Let the Journey Begin,
Dr. Dwayne L. Buckingham

Marriage Sustainment Strategy #1

Communicate to Create Harmony

Make It Last Forever:

If you talk *at* your spouse, he or she will shut down. However, if you talk *with* your spouse, he or she will open up. Two-way dialogue is the most effective manner for gaining understanding and insight into marital challenges.

You at work:

Talk with your spouse, not at him or her. Remember that effective communication is the key to marital bliss and longevity. By doing this work, you will be better equipped to address and resolve challenges early, thus making your marriage last forever.

Write your plan of action here:

_____

_____

_____

_____

_____

_____

_____

_____

Marriage Sustainment Strategy #2

Give Attention to Get Attention

Make It Last Forever:

Show interest in order to demonstrate fondness and consideration.

You at work:

In order to get attention, show interest in things that are important to your spouse. By doing this work, you will be more knowledgeable about the things that are important to your spouse. Shared interests contribute to harmonious interactions, thus making your marriage last forever.

Write your plan of action here:

_____

_____

_____

_____

_____

_____

_____

_____

_____

Marriage Sustainment Strategy #3

Enjoy Your Spouse

Make It Last Forever:

Engage in enjoyable activities with a shared purpose in order to build a purposeful marriage.

You at work:

Develop and engage in activities that you both enjoy (cooking, working-out, singing, running a business, volunteering, etc.). By doing this work, you will share meaningful experiences with your spouse, thus making your marriage last forever.

Write your plan of action here:

_____

_____

_____

_____

_____

_____

_____

_____

_____

_____

Marriage Sustainment Strategy #4

Rekindle the Fire

Make It Last Forever:

You are one in marriage because you spent time becoming one. In order to remain as one, you must strive to rekindle the fire that once burned. Repeat the behaviors that got you to the altar.

You at work:

Schedule "couple time" outside of "family time." Focusing attention on your spouse demonstrates that you care about his or her needs. By doing this work, you will feel rejuvenated and motivated to please your spouse, thus making your marriage last forever.

Write your plan of action here:

_____

_____

_____

_____

_____

_____

_____

_____

Marriage Sustainment Strategy #5

Be Creative

Make It Last Forever:

We all get excited about new things, especially if the new things are pleasing to us. Change is difficult, but can be very rewarding. Your marriage can be your creative zone.

You at work:

Try new things sexually, physically and emotionally. Change your routines and your marriage will change. By doing this work, you will keep your spouse curious and excited, thus making your marriage last forever.

Write your plan of action here:

_____

_____

_____

_____

_____

_____

_____

_____

_____

Marriage Sustainment Strategy #6

Validate Emotions

Make It Last Forever:

The root cause of most marital conflict is the invalidation of emotions. How a person feels is real to him or her. This is why you must validate emotions.

You at work:

The quickest way to resolve emotional distress is to recognize and respect it. This does not mean that you will always understand or agree with your spouse's emotions; simply validate them. By doing this work, you will feel more connected to your spouse. Emotions drive behavior. If you recognize emotions, you will experience less drama, thus making your marriage last forever.

Write your plan of action here:

_____

_____

_____

_____

_____

_____

Marriage Sustainment Strategy #7

Manage Perceptions

Make It Last Forever:

Know that your spouse might defend his or her perceptions even if they are incorrect. Manage perceptions by understanding that a person's perception is his or her reality. Do not disregard your spouse's perceptions. Listen so you can try to provide clarity.

You at work:

Recognize and address your spouse's perceptions. Do not argue about perceptions, instead recognize them and work to resolve incorrect perceptions. By doing this work, you will minimize power struggles and prevent intense arguments, thus making your marriage last forever.

Write your plan of action here:

_____

_____

_____

_____

_____

_____

_____

Marriage Sustainment Strategy #8

Maintain a Positive Mental Image

Make It Last Forever:

Actively engage and train your mind to see the positive aspects of your spouse and marriage.

You at work:

Schedule positive reflection time and identify five things you really love about your spouse. Spend time reflecting on them. By doing this work, you will be conditioned to hold your spouse in high-esteem during good and bad times, thus making your marriage last forever.

Write your plan of action here:

_____

_____

_____

_____

_____

_____

_____

_____

_____

_____

Marriage Sustainment Strategy #9

Grow and Learn Together

Make It Last Forever:

Attend a marriage enhancement seminar with your spouse.

You at work:

Develop a plan to implement what you learned in the seminar. Teamwork is critical in marriage because individuals need to feel that their opinion matters. By doing this work you will receive mutual buy-in and be able to steer your marriage in a direction you both agree on, thus making your marriage last forever.

Write your plan of action here:

_____
_____
_____
_____
_____
_____
_____
_____
_____
_____
_____
_____
_____
_____

Marriage Sustainment Strategy #10

Make Love Work, Not Hurt

Make It Last Forever:

Be mindful that degrading, belittling or making your spouse feel powerless or worthless is counter-productive to having a healthy marriage. Avoid name-calling and insults. Remember that true love cannot be forced and it should not hurt.

You at work:

Avoid all forms of abuse: emotional, physical, sexual or spiritual. By doing this work, you will demonstrate ultimate respect for your spouse, thus making your marriage last forever.

Write your plan of action here:

_____

_____

_____

_____

_____

_____

_____

_____

_____

_____

_____

_____

Marriage Sustainment Strategy #11

Respect Personal Time

Make It Last Forever:

There are three components in every marriage: you, me and us. Remember that your spouse had a life before you. One of the biggest challenges for couples is to learn that each person must have time to address personal needs.

You at work:

Respect the need for personal time. By doing this work, your spouse will not feel smothered, thus making your marriage last forever.

Write your plan of action here:

_____

_____

_____

_____

_____

_____

_____

_____

_____

_____

_____

_____

_____

_____

_____

Marriage Sustainment Strategy #12

Make the Most of Your Time

Make It Last Forever:

Quantity is not the same as quality. Existing in the same house equates to quantity time, but does not necessarily equate to quality. Meaningful interactions and conversations fall in the realm of quality time. Make the most of your time – stay connected.

You at Work:

Spend quality time with your spouse. By doing this work, you will never lose sight of why you fell in love, thus making your marriage last forever.

Write your plan of action here:

_____
_____
_____
_____
_____
_____
_____
_____
_____
_____
_____
_____
_____
_____

Marriage Sustainment Strategy #13

Connect in Multiple Ways

Make It Last Forever:

Marriages blossom when individuals connect in multiple ways and strive to create life-time harmony.

You at work:

Bond with your spouse emotionally, physically and spiritually. By doing this work, you will create an unbreakable bond, thus making your marriage last forever.

Write your plan of action here:

_____
_____
_____
_____
_____
_____
_____
_____
_____
_____
_____
_____
_____
_____
_____
_____
_____
_____

Marriage Sustainment Strategy #14

Remain Supportive

Make It Last Forever:

Demonstrate patience, respect and common courtesy.

You at work:

Support your spouse's educational, professional and personal goals. Every desire or idea is worth discussing. Hear him or her out before you make a decision or pass judgment. By doing this work, you will enable your spouse to speak freely with you without fear or hesitation, thus making your marriage last forever.

Write your plan of action here:

_____
_____
_____
_____
_____
_____
_____
_____
_____
_____
_____
_____
_____

Marriage Sustainment Strategy #15

Do Not Break Trust

Make It Last Forever:

Discontinue behaviors that cause your spouse to question your trustworthiness. If there is a significant amount of distress associated with certain actions; simply discontinue them, for example, talking to or meeting with an old "flame or ex." Strive to maintain trust.

You at work:

Develop and maintain a trusting marriage. If you have a problem with trusting yourself or your spouse, please meditate on the following scriptures: Proverbs 3:5 – "Trust in the Lord with all your heart, and do not lean on your own understanding"; and Jeremiah 29:11- "For I know the plans I have for you, declares the Lord, plans for welfare and not for evil, to give you a future and a hope." By doing this work, you will make it close to impossible to destroy your scarce bond, thus making your marriage last forever.

Write your plan of action here:

_____

_____

_____

_____

_____

_____

_____

_____

Marriage Sustainment Strategy #16

Keep Positive Company

Make It Last Forever:

Interact with friends and family members who support your marriage and have positive things to contribute. Remember misery loves miserable company.

You at work:

Be mindful of the people with whom you socialize and make sure that they want what is best for you and your spouse. By doing this work, you will eliminate negative energy and people from your life, thus making your marriage last forever.

Write your plan of action here:

_____
_____
_____
_____
_____
_____
_____
_____
_____
_____
_____
_____
_____
_____

Marriage Sustainment Strategy #17

Be Accountable for Self

Make It Last Forever:

Remember that no one is responsible for you, but you. Your spouse can contribute to your emotional state, but cannot cause or determine it. Don't blame others when you exercise your free will.

You at work:

Be responsible for your actions and words. By doing this work, you will make it easier for your spouse to respect you, thus making your marriage last forever.

Write your plan of action here:

_____

_____

_____

_____

_____

_____

_____

_____

_____

_____

_____

_____

_____

_____

Marriage Sustainment Strategy #18

Manage Conflict Effectively

Make It Last Forever:

You can disagree with your spouse without being disrespectful.

You at work:

Learn to agree to disagree. Conflict is not bad unless you cope with it ineffectively. By doing this work, you will create an environment that is free of negative tension and energy, thus making your marriage last forever.

Write your plan of action here:

_____

_____

_____

_____

_____

_____

_____

_____

_____

_____

_____

_____

_____

_____

_____

_____

_____

Marriage Sustainment Strategy #19

Maintain Your Friendship

Make It Last Forever:

You should treat your spouse like your best friend. Do not withhold information and do give unconditional support. Reflect on the conversations and moments you shared as friends. Make your spouse feel wanted.

You at work:

Build on the friendship you initially established when you first courted. By doing this work, you will view your spouse as a lover *and* a friend, thus making your marriage last forever.

Write your plan of action here:

_____
_____
_____
_____
_____
_____
_____
_____
_____
_____
_____
_____
_____
_____

Marriage Sustainment Strategy #20

Use Positive and Uplifting Words

Make It Last Forever:

Words of kindness please the heart and soul. Gifts are nice, but do not have the same effect as kind words. Apologize with words. Inspire with words. Empower with words.

You at work:

Use your tongue as an empowering and motivational tool. By doing this work you will enhance your spouse's self-esteem, thus making your marriage last forever.

Write your plan of action here:

_____
_____
_____
_____
_____
_____
_____
_____
_____
_____
_____
_____
_____
_____
_____
_____

Marriage Sustainment Strategy #21

Monitor Your Pride and Attitude

Make It Last Forever:

Too much pride is unhealthy and can prevent you from humbling yourself. Arrogant individuals see the value in themselves. In contrast, humble individuals see the value in themselves *and* their spouses.

You at work:

Eliminate prideful attitudes and practice humbleness. By doing this work you will be able to see the value in your spouse, thus marking your marriage last forever.

Write your plan of action here:

_____
_____
_____
_____
_____
_____
_____
_____
_____
_____
_____
_____
_____

Marriage Sustainment Strategy #22

Be a Team Player

Make It Last Forever:

Empower your spouse to actively participate in decisions that affect the both of you. Marriage works well when two individuals are on the same page and are striving to accomplish the same goal.

You at work:

Be a team player. Share responsibility for making decisions in your marriage. By doing this work you will get the best out of your spouse, thus making your marriage last forever.

Write your plan of action here:

_____

_____

_____

_____

_____

_____

_____

_____

_____

_____

_____

_____

_____

_____

_____

Marriage Sustainment Strategy #23

Maintain Balance

Make It Last Forever:

Sharing of tasks can potentially prevent burnout. Individuals who are suffering from burnout or physical and emotional exhaustion are more likely to function in an unproductive and unhealthy manner.

You at work:

Give your spouse some help. Divide household chores and parental responsibilities. By doing this work you will benefit from an energized and rejuvenated spouse, thus making your marriage last forever.

Write your plan of action here:

_____

_____

_____

_____

_____

_____

_____

_____

_____

_____

_____

_____

_____

_____

Marriage Sustainment Strategy #24

Show and Express Your Gratitude

Make It Last Forever:

Demonstrate your fondness and gratitude through your actions.

You at work:

Do little things to show how happy you are to be with your spouse. Let your spouse know that you are proud to be with him or her. By doing this work, you will reap what you sow, thus making your marriage last forever.

Write your plan of action here:

_____
_____
_____
_____
_____
_____
_____
_____
_____
_____
_____
_____
_____
_____
_____

Marriage Sustainment Strategy #25

Assert Yourself

Make It Last Forever:

Your spouse may or may not be aware of his or her attitude or behavior. Never assume anything. Assumptions contribute to poor communication.

You at work:

Assertively express your concerns and give your spouse a chance to explain him or herself. Discuss perceived or actual changes in attitudes or behavior. By doing this work, you will avoid the passive/aggressive trap, thus making your marriage last forever.

Write your plan of action here:

_____
_____
_____
_____
_____
_____
_____
_____
_____
_____
_____
_____
_____
_____

Marriage Sustainment Strategy #26

Breathe Life into Your Spouse

Make It Last Forever:

Each person has something valuable to contribute to the marriage. Your spouse said "I do," believing that you would be there for him or her through the good and bad and until death do you part. Given this, it is your Godly obligation to inspire, encourage and motivate your spouse.

You at work:

Do not diminish your spouse's worth or value. Be the air that he or she needs to thrive and survive. By doing this work, you will help your spouse live with a renewed purpose, thus making your marriage last forever.

Write your plan of action here:

_____

_____

_____

_____

_____

_____

_____

_____

_____

_____

_____

_____

Marriage Sustainment Strategy #27

Avoid Making Character Attacks

Make It Last Forever:

Attacking character flaws contributes to feelings of anger, defensiveness and frustration. Individuals can work on their behavior more easily than their character flaws.

You at work:

Describe desired changes in behavior, not character. Focus on and address behavior, not character flaws. By doing this work, you will prevent your spouse from becoming defensive and bitter, thus making your marriage last forever.

Write your plan of action here:

_____

_____

_____

_____

_____

_____

_____

_____

_____

_____

_____

_____

_____

_____

Marriage Sustainment Strategy #28

Offer Positive Criticism

Make It Last Forever:

If you desire change, build up your spouse's spirit by making positive statements. Criticism is only bad when it diminishes worth.

You at work:

Find helpful and productive ways to get the best out of your spouse. Do not constantly remind your spouse of his or her imperfections. By doing this work, you will help build confidence and eagerness, thus making your marriage last forever.

Write your plan of action here:

_____

_____

_____

_____

_____

_____

_____

_____

_____

_____

_____

_____

_____

_____

Marriage Sustainment Strategy #29

Exhibit Unwavering Commitment

Make It Last Forever:

Demonstrate willingness to stay through the good and the bad. Cry and laugh with him or her. Stand by his or her side when faced with adversity. Let your spouse know that your mood might change, but your commitment will not.

You at work:

Let your spouse know that you are committed to him or her and the marriage. By doing this work, you will develop an unbreakable bond with your spouse, thus making your marriage last forever.

Write your plan of action here:

_____

_____

_____

_____

_____

_____

_____

_____

_____

_____

_____

_____

_____

Marriage Sustainment Strategy #30

Give and Express Love Consistently

Make It Last Forever:

Love him or her when he or she is happy, sad, angry or depressed. There is no such thing as perfect love, but there is faithful love.

You at work:

Be faithful and consistent with your love. Do not ration or allocate love based on your spouse's behavior or mood. By doing this work, you will demonstrate a pattern of consistent and unwavering love, thus making your marriage last forever.

Write your plan of action here:

_____

_____

_____

_____

_____

_____

_____

_____

_____

_____

_____

_____

_____

_____

Marriage Sustainment Strategy #31

Build-Up or Remain Silent

Make It Last Forever:

Provide constructive advice or suggestions to your spouse. If you do not have something constructive to say, do not say anything at all.

You at work:

Be a vessel for inspiration and growth or be a silent observer if you cannot be helpful. By doing this work, you will be better positioned to influence your spouse's behavior, thus making your marriage last forever.

Write your plan of action here:

_____

_____

_____

_____

_____

_____

_____

_____

_____

_____

_____

_____

_____

Marriage Sustainment Strategy #32

Minimize Intellectualization

Make It Last Forever:

Intellectualizing does not allow you to cope with or address the emotional distress you or your spouse experience. Address underlying emotional stressors in your marriage in order to get to the source of discomfort. Minimize intellectualization of stressors in your marriage.

You at work:

Be mindful that intellectualization is a defense mechanism where reasoning is used to block confrontation with an unconscious conflict and its associated emotional stress. Removing yourself emotionally from a stressful event does not make the event any less stressful. Do not use thinking to avoid feeling. By doing this work, you will be better equipped to deal with emotionally charged conflict, thus making your marriage last forever.

Write your plan of action here:

_____

_____

_____

_____

_____

_____

_____

_____

_____

Marriage Sustainment Strategy #33

Have Sex Regularly

Make It Last Forever:

While sexual frustration is not the primary reason for extra-marital affairs, it can contribute to infidelity if emotional frustrations are also present. Emotional detachment combined with physical detachment is not good for relationships.

You at work:

Be mindful that some individuals express their love by means of physical and sexual affection. Do not deny your spouse sexual pleasure. By doing this work, you will minimize the risk of infidelity, thus making your marriage last forever.

Write your plan of action here:

_____

_____

_____

_____

_____

_____

_____

_____

_____

_____

_____

_____

_____

Marriage Sustainment Strategy #34

Resolve Anger and Resentment

Make It Last Forever:

Understand that built up and unresolved anger and resentment can penetrate every aspect of your marriage. Discuss your anger and resentment early and seek counseling if you cannot resolve these issues.

You at work:

Deal with your anger and resentment or both emotions will deal with you. Anger and resentment are two of the most poorly managed emotions. Do not allow them to build up and create problems in your marriage. By doing this work, you will prevent the negative snow-ball effect, thus making your marriage last forever.

Write your plan of action here:

_____

_____

_____

_____

_____

_____

_____

_____

_____

_____

_____

_____

_____

Marriage Sustainment Strategy #35

Speak in a Respectful Manner

Make It Last Forever:

Ask politely and allow your spouse sufficient time to respond to your request. It is okay to be assertive, but not disrespectful.

You at work:

Be as specific as possible about your request, but not demanding. Never command, direct or order your spouse to do anything. By doing this work, you will experience increased openness and agreement, thus making your marriage last forever.

Write your plan of action here:

_____

_____

_____

_____

_____

_____

_____

_____

_____

_____

_____

_____

_____

_____

Marriage Sustainment Strategy #36

Be Solution Focused

Make It Last Forever:

Offer solutions to problems instead of nagging without providing viable options.

You at work:

Help move your marriage forward. By doing this work, you will feel more empowered to have the kind of marriage that you desire, thus making your marriage last forever.

Write your plan of action here:

_____
_____
_____
_____
_____
_____
_____
_____
_____
_____
_____
_____
_____
_____
_____

Marriage Sustainment Strategy #37

Put Everything on the Table

Make It Last Forever:

Learn to face adversity head on, instead of allowing it to resurface later.

You at work:

Avoid withdrawing, diverting or humoring in order to circumvent emotional discomfort. By doing this work, you will prevent things from snowballing, thus making your marriage last forever.

Write your plan of action here:

_____
_____
_____
_____
_____
_____
_____
_____
_____
_____
_____
_____
_____
_____
_____
_____

Marriage Sustainment Strategy #38

Pick Your Battles Wisely

Make It Last Forever:

Learn to address what is affecting you considerably and be willing to compromise to get your needs met.

You at work:

Don't complain about everything your spouse does or doesn't do. By doing this work, you will experience less stress and frustration, thus making your marriage last forever.

Write your plan of action here:

_____
_____
_____
_____
_____
_____
_____
_____
_____
_____
_____
_____
_____
_____
_____

Marriage Sustainment Strategy #39

Breathe Life into Your Marriage

Make It Last Forever:

Develop helpful habits that will nurture your marriage and allow it to grow. Think positively, remain calm and be flexible. Create an environment in which it is difficult for your spouse to breathe without you.

You at work:

Practice and live by the Golden Rule. If it is good enough for you, it should be good enough for your spouse. By doing this work, you will convince your spouse to believe that marrying you was the best decision he or she has ever made.

Write your plan of action here:

_____
_____
_____
_____
_____
_____
_____
_____
_____
_____
_____
_____
_____
_____
_____

Marriage Sustainment Strategy #40

Stay Focused on Your Marriage

Make It Last Forever:

Your marriage is unique. Your circumstances might mirror others, but no two couples have exactly the same problems or coping skills. Identify the strengths and weaknesses in your marriage and use these strengths to address your weaknesses.

You at work:

Don't compare your marriage to other people's marriage— not your parents' marriage, best friend's marriage or anyone else. By doing this work, you will maintain a realistic view of your marriage and be able to work through your own lens, thus making your marriage last forever.

Write your plan of action here:

_____
_____
_____
_____
_____
_____
_____
_____
_____
_____
_____
_____

Marriage Sustainment Strategy #41

Practice Team Parenting

Make It Last Forever:

Be consistent and reinforce each other's efforts. Do not rely solely on your childhood experience, especially if it differs considerably from your spouse's. Eradicate conflict in childrearing practices by working as a team.

You at work:

Be supportive of each other's efforts regarding childrearing. Frustration surrounding appropriate childrearing can cause relational conflict. By doing this work, you will prevent your child or children from splitting, thus making your marriage last forever.

Write your plan of action here:

_____
_____
_____
_____
_____
_____
_____
_____
_____
_____
_____
_____
_____

Marriage Sustainment Strategy #42

Live and Stand by Your Word

Make It Last Forever:

Do as you say and keep your promises.

You at work:

Say what you mean and mean what you say. Don't leave room for mistrust to sneak into your marriage. By doing this work, you will be able to establish and maintain trust with your spouse, thus making your marriage last forever.

Write your plan of action here:

_____
_____
_____
_____
_____
_____
_____
_____
_____
_____
_____
_____
_____
_____
_____
_____
_____

Marriage Sustainment Strategy #43

Speak Through Your Action

Make It Last Forever:

Your spouse will pay closer attention to what you do than to what you say. Therefore, you should behave in a manner that eliminates doubt and leaves a lasting and respectable impression on your spouse.

You at work:

Remember that actions speak louder than words. By doing this work, you will never be questioned or second guessed by your spouse, thus making your marriage last forever.

Write your plan of action here:

_____
_____
_____
_____
_____
_____
_____
_____
_____
_____
_____
_____
_____

Marriage Sustainment Strategy #44

Become a Strategist

Make It Last Forever:

Put on your thinking cap before you respond. No one is perfect, but everyone is teachable. Strategize and view flaws as opportunities for growth.

You at work:

Help your spouse identify shortcomings and work with him or her to correct them. By doing this work, you will empower your spouse, thus making your marriage last forever.

Write your plan of action here:

_____

_____

_____

_____

_____

_____

_____

_____

_____

_____

_____

_____

Marriage Sustainment Strategy #45

Examine Yourself

Make It Last Forever:

It is very difficult to confront or help someone else when you yourself are unhealthy or troubled. Take care of yourself and your troubles will not intensify. Self-awareness and personal accountability is more attractive than attacking and blaming.

You at work:

Exhibit the behavior you desire in return. Seek to understand and address your own problems before you attempt to tackle your spouse's problems. Acknowledge and vocalize your challenges. By doing this work, you will be better positioned to see the kind of change you desire, thus making your marriage last forever.

Write your plan of action here:

_____
_____
_____
_____
_____
_____
_____
_____
_____
_____
_____
_____
_____

Marriage Sustainment Strategy #46

Respect Your Spouse's Uniqueness

Make It Last Forever:

Do not expect your significant other to cope with life problems the way you do. What affects you may not affect your significant other in the same manner.

You at work:

Allow for and encourage personal exploration and coping. Remember that no two people are the same. Uniqueness should be valued and respected. Appreciate differences and learn to capitalize from them. By doing this work, your mind will be open to different perspectives and views, thus making your marriage last forever.

Write your plan of action here:

_____
_____
_____
_____
_____
_____
_____
_____
_____
_____
_____
_____
_____

Marriage Sustainment Strategy #47

Think Prevention

Make It Last Forever:

Understand that an ounce of prevention is worth a pound of cure.

You at work:

Increase your awareness of relationship stressors and work to prevent them before they become unmanageable. By doing this work, you will experience less distress, thus making your marriage last forever.

Write your plan of action here:

_____
_____
_____
_____
_____
_____
_____
_____
_____
_____
_____
_____
_____
_____
_____
_____
_____

Marriage Sustainment Strategy #48

Get Buy-In

Make It Last Forever:

Avoid making lifestyle, financial or other significant changes that affect your spouse without his or her approval. Listening to your spouse helps him or her feel important.

You at work:

Be mindful that two heads are better than one. Your spouse may have a perspective that is critical to the decision-making process. People value things that they believe in and support. By doing this work, you will be positioned to tackle life with a shared vision and motivation, thus making your marriage last forever.

Write your plan of action here:

_____
_____
_____
_____
_____
_____
_____
_____
_____
_____
_____
_____
_____
_____

Marriage Sustainment Strategy #49

Change Self-Preserving Behaviors

Make It Last Forever:

Marriage is a union, not an individualized relationship. Eliminate things that create division and disagreement. For example, you should consider getting rid of your individual bank account if your spouse has expressed disapproval and has closed his' or her's.

You at work:

Identify and eliminate self-preserving behaviors that are not good for your marriage. By doing this work, you will feel more connected to your spouse, thus making your marriage last forever.

Write your plan of action here:

_____

_____

_____

_____

_____

_____

_____

_____

_____

_____

_____

_____

Marriage Sustainment Strategy #50

Resolve Control Issues

Make It Last Forever:

Learn to relax and take the backseat occasionally. Demonstrate trust in your spouse and remember that God gave everyone the gift of free will. Your spouse is going to do what he or she is going to do.

You at work:

Turn your worries to God and let go. Do away with your need to be in control of yourself or your significant other all the time. This is stress-provoking and will cause your relationship to suffer. No one likes to be controlled. By doing this work, you will experience less anxiety and fear, thus making your marriage last forever.

Write your plan of action here:

_____
_____
_____
_____
_____
_____
_____
_____
_____
_____
_____
_____

Marriage Sustainment Strategy #51

Avoid the Scapegoat Syndrome

Make It Last Forever:

Find means to cope with your frustration instead of unloading on your spouse.

You at work:

Use your spouse as a support system, not a scapegoat or target. Do not transfer your life, occupational or family stressors on to your spouse. Do not make your spouse your scapegoat. By doing this work, you will create a life-long and supportive union, thus making your marriage last forever.

Write your plan of action here:

_____

_____

_____

_____

_____

_____

_____

_____

_____

_____

_____

_____

_____

Marriage Sustainment Strategy #52

Praise Your Spouse

Make It Last Forever:

The journey towards marital excellence is a tough road to travel without proper praise.

You at work:

Be encouraging. Get rid of perfectionist attitudes and praise your spouse for doing his or her best. By doing this work, you keep your spouse motivated and inspired to face challenges with confidence, thus making your marriage last forever.

Write your plan of action here:

_____
_____
_____
_____
_____
_____
_____
_____
_____
_____
_____
_____
_____

Marriage Sustainment Strategy #53

Delay Gratification

Make It Last Forever:

Remember that patience is a virtue. God does not always give us what we need when we need it, but He always delivers. Be mindful that good things come to those who wait.

You at work:

Delay immediate gratification and work to save your marriage. Be patient and learn to control your need for immediate satisfaction and pleasure. By doing this work, you will learn discipline and sacrifice, thus making your marriage last forever.

Write your plan of action here:

_____

_____

_____

_____

_____

_____

_____

_____

_____

_____

_____

_____

_____

Marriage Sustainment Strategy #54

Take Time-Outs

Make It Last Forever:

Schedule time to address heated or tense issues. Do not have conversations if you are or your spouse is emotionally charged.

You at work:

Utilize time-outs. Take a break to calm down before discussions get heated and become unproductive. Follow up after everyone is composed. By doing this work, you will avoid saying and doing things you regret, thus making your marriage last forever.

Write your plan of action here:

_____
_____
_____
_____
_____
_____
_____
_____
_____
_____
_____
_____
_____
_____

Marriage Sustainment Strategy #55

Hold Your Spouse Accountable

Make It Last Forever:

Accountability is the key to growth in your marriage. If your spouse behaves inappropriately, do not complain if you do not address the behavior.

You at work:

Do not take personal responsibility for the actions of your spouse. Take action early and do not stack pile issues. Hold spouse accountable. By doing this work, you will eliminate victim thinking and behavior, thus making your marriage last forever.

Write your plan of action here:

_____

_____

_____

_____

_____

_____

_____

_____

_____

_____

_____

_____

_____

_____

Marriage Sustainment Strategy #56

Avoid Mood-Altering Substances

Make It Last Forever:

Absolutely do not engage in important or sensitive conversations if you have or your spouse has consumed alcohol or any other mood-altering substances. Alcohol and other substances lower self-consciousness and cause people say and do things that they regret later.

You at work:

Avoid any substance that alters your mood. If you can't handle the outcome, do not use the substance. By doing this work, you will be in control, thus making your marriage last forever.

Write your plan of action here:

_____
_____
_____
_____
_____
_____
_____
_____
_____
_____
_____
_____
_____

Marriage Sustainment Strategy #57

Manage Stress through Exercise

Make It Last Forever:

Exercise is good for your physical and emotional health. It reduces the level of stress in your body. Taking care of your mind and body should be a priority.

You at work:

Work off some of your relationship frustration or stress with physical exercise. By doing this work, you will be better prepared to handle relationship stress more effectively, thus making your marriage last forever.

Write your plan of action here:

_____
_____
_____
_____
_____
_____
_____
_____
_____
_____
_____
_____
_____

Marriage Sustainment Strategy #58

Maintain a Conqueror's Mentality

Make It Last Forever:

If you believe you can win, you will. However, don't forget you win *together*.

You at work:

Equip yourself with healthy coping tools and prepare for battle. Think of marital stress as a challenge to be conquered. Victory is yours if you believe it. By doing this work, you will feel hopeful when faced with relationship adversity, thus making your marriage last forever.

Write your plan of action here:

_____
_____
_____
_____
_____
_____
_____
_____
_____
_____
_____
_____
_____
_____
_____

Marriage Sustainment Strategy #59

Seek Professional Guidance

Make It Last Forever:

Family and friends are a great source of support, but they frequently struggle with objectivity. Sometimes you need to hear what is *good* for you, not what you want to hear.

You at work:

Talk with family for supportive purposes and speak with professionals for guidance. Follow the guidance of knowledgeable, objective and unbiased professionals. By doing this work, you will eliminate subjective opinions and drama from entering your marriage, thus making it last forever.

Write your plan of action here:

_____

_____

_____

_____

_____

_____

_____

_____

_____

_____

_____

_____

_____

_____

Marriage Sustainment Strategy #60

Do Right by Your Spouse

Make It Last Forever:

Do not live with an eye-for-eye mentality. Do not engage in destructive or inappropriate behavior because your spouse does. Remember the old saying, "two wrongs don't make a right."

You at work:

Know that life and love is not always fair, but God is. Do right by your spouse regardless of how he or she treats you. By doing this work, you will live with your integrity and self-respect intact, thus making your marriage last forever.

Write your plan of action here:

_____

_____

_____

_____

_____

_____

_____

_____

_____

_____

_____

_____

_____

Marriage Sustainment Strategy #61

Connect with God

Make It Last Forever:

Individuals who believe in a Higher Power typically attempt to cope with marital distress in a positive manner. Prayer and meditation can reduce personal stress and enhance your relationship.

You at work:

Establish a spiritual relationship with God. By doing this work, you will be able to cope with feelings of defeat in an optimistic and productive manner, thus making your marriage last forever.

Write your plan of action here:

_____

_____

_____

_____

_____

_____

_____

_____

_____

_____

_____

_____

_____

_____

Marriage Sustainment Strategy #62

Learn to Relax

Make It Last Forever:

Relaxation helps neutralize stress chemicals in your body. Reducing stress and worrying less can enhance your emotional and physical well-being.

You at work:

Develop a relaxation plan that involves deep breathing, progressive muscle relaxation and guided imagery. By doing this work, you will feel rejuvenated in your marriage, thus making it last forever.

Write your plan of action here:

_____
_____
_____
_____
_____
_____
_____
_____
_____
_____
_____
_____
_____
_____

Marriage Sustainment Strategy #63

Avoid Playing Mind Games

Make It Last Forever:

You cannot have a healthy marriage if you try to take advantage of your spouse's weaknesses or shortcomings. They say that a mind is terrible thing to waste, but so is a marriage.

You at work:

Avoid psychological warfare at all cost. Your spouse is to be loved, not to be manipulated mentally. By doing this work, your spouse will not feel anxious or fearful, thus making your marriage last forever.

Write your plan of action here:

_____

_____

_____

_____

_____

_____

_____

_____

_____

_____

_____

_____

_____

Marriage Sustainment Strategy #64

Show Your Vulnerability

Make It Last Forever:

Do not act like you are strong all the time or do not care when you really do. Insecurities let your spouse know that you have vulnerabilities and that you will occasionally need reassurance. Arrogance will destroy you and your marriage.

You at work:

Acknowledge and vocalize your insecurities. By doing this work, you will foster compassion and eliminate the need for mind-reading, thus making your marriage last forever.

Write your plan of action here:

_____

_____

_____

_____

_____

_____

_____

_____

_____

_____

_____

_____

_____

_____

Marriage Sustainment Strategy #65

Seek Spiritual Counsel

Make It Last Forever:

Pray daily and seek out spiritual leaders who can counsel you if your marriage becomes intensely stressful. Spiritual counseling is a tool to be used for healing purposes and to enhance your faith in the power of God.

You at work:

Seek spiritual guidance in order to keep your marriage grounded. By doing this work, you will gain renewed faith in your spouse and marriage, thus making it last forever.

Write your plan of action here:

_____
_____
_____
_____
_____
_____
_____
_____
_____
_____
_____
_____
_____
_____
_____

Marriage Sustainment Strategy #66

Get Help

Make It Last Forever:

Seek professional help if you or your spouse experience frequent loss of emotional control or begin to withdrawal from each other.

You at work:

Don't be afraid to ask for and seek help. Do not get discouraged about things that can be addressed through professional guidance. Always be willing to receive counsel. By doing this work, you will acquire the tools needed to be a loving spouse, thus making your marriage last forever.

Write your plan of action here:

_____

_____

_____

_____

_____

_____

_____

_____

_____

_____

_____

_____

_____

Marriage Sustainment Strategy #67

Maintain a Heart of Forgiveness

Make It Last Forever:

What is done is done. Move forward or move on. God requires us to forgive thus who trespass against us.

You at work:

Do not rehash unpleasant events. Energy that is used on unpleasant events is wasted energy. Create positive energy in your marriage by maintaining a heart of forgiveness. Write a letter of forgiveness if you are not good with words. Seeking forgiveness demonstrates feelings of remorsefulness and lets your spouse know that you care about his or her feelings. By doing this work, you will feel more at peace, thus making your marriage last forever.

Write your plan of action here:

_____

_____

_____

_____

_____

_____

_____

_____

_____

_____

_____

Marriage Sustainment Strategy #68

Exercise Your Free Will Wisely

Make It Last Forever:

Exercise your *free will* for the betterment of your marriage.

You at work:

God gave you the gift of free will and no one can take it away. However, it is imperative that you realize that your actions and decisions can and do impact your marriage. Free will is a beautiful thing, especially when it is used to enhance your marriage. Always chose to do what is best for you and your spouse when possible. By doing this work, you will never devalue your spouse, thus making your marriage last forever.

Write your plan of action here:

_____

_____

_____

_____

_____

_____

_____

_____

_____

_____

_____

_____

Marriage Sustainment Strategy #69

Be "We" Focused

Make It Last Forever:

Remember that no one likes to talk with individuals who spend the majority of their time talking about themselves and their needs. Your spouse agreed to marriage with the hope that the two of you would complement each other and build a "we" empire.

You at work:

Minimize or eliminate the use of "I" talk from your conversations and incorporate some "we" talk. By doing this work, you will honor your vows and build a spirit of cooperation, thus making your marriage last forever.

Write your plan of action here:

_____

_____

_____

_____

_____

_____

_____

_____

_____

_____

_____

_____

_____

Marriage Sustainment Strategy #70

Be the Best You

Make It Last Forever:

Strive to give the best in your marriage. Good relationships exist because of the work that individuals put into them.

You at work:

View each day as a new opportunity to do something positive that will elevate your marriage to a new level. Work to be the best you and encourage your spouse to do the same. By doing this work, you can learn from your shortcomings and turn them into successes, thus making your marriage last forever.

Write your plan of action here:

_____

_____

_____

_____

_____

_____

_____

_____

_____

_____

_____

_____

_____

Marriage Sustainment Strategy #71

Understand Money

Make It Last Forever:

Money is not the root of all evil; people are. Money can buy a lot of things, but it cannot buy unconditional love.

You at work:

Never make your spouse feel trapped or belittled because of money. Love of money is not bad, but monetary wealth will never satisfy the need for belonging and affection. Use money to enhance your marriage, not control it. Put your spouse in the center of your life, not money. By doing this work, your spouse will realize that he or she is more important than money, thus making your marriage last forever.

Write your plan of action here:

_____

_____

_____

_____

_____

_____

_____

_____

_____

_____

_____

_____

Marriage Sustainment Strategy #72

Apply the Golden Rule

Make It Last Forever:

"Do unto your spouse as you would have him or her do unto you." – Matthew 7:12.

You at work:

Apply the Golden Rule in your marriage. Practice tolerance, consideration and compassion. By doing this work, you will be more mindful of how you want to be treated, thus making your marriage last forever.

Write your plan of action here:

_____

_____

_____

_____

_____

_____

_____

_____

_____

_____

_____

_____

_____

Marriage Sustainment Strategy #73

Use Positive Affirmations

Make It Last Forever:

Self-talk is a powerful tool so use it wisely. Use positive affirmations to help you cope with difficult situations in your marriage.

You at work:

Promote the use of positive affirmations in your marriage and make positive statements on a daily basis. For example, "I am capable of dealing with anything I put my mind to." By doing this work, you will make progressive moves in your marriage, thus making it last forever.

Write your plan of action here:

_____
_____
_____
_____
_____
_____
_____
_____
_____
_____
_____
_____
_____
_____
_____
_____

Marriage Sustainment Strategy #74

Set Attainable Marital Goals

Make It Last Forever:

Measurable and realistic goals can lead to increased marital satisfaction when accomplished.

You at work:

Do not live your life hoping that things will get better. Be action-oriented and create the marriage you desire. Set attainable marriage goals such as reducing arguments or conflicts from five times a week to three times a week. No arguing is the ultimate goal, but reduced arguing is the attainable goal. By doing this work, you will have something to work toward, thus making your marriage last forever.

Write your plan of action here:

_____

_____

_____

_____

_____

_____

_____

_____

_____

_____

_____

Marriage Sustainment Strategy #75

Enhance Your Compromising Skills

Make It Last Forever:

Learn to compromise and express your interests, preferences and expectations in a non-aggressive manner. Assertiveness can facilitate positive communication by reducing defensiveness in your spouse.

You at work:

Enhance your negotiation and compromising skills by attending assertiveness training. Know that you have to be willing to give a little in order to get a little. By doing this work, you will create win-win situations for both you and your spouse, thus making your marriage last forever.

Write your plan of action here:

_____

_____

_____

_____

_____

_____

_____

_____

_____

_____

_____

_____

Marriage Sustainment Strategy #76

Develop an Incentive Contract

Make It Last Forever:

Develop and use an incentive contract in your marriage.

You at work:

Work with your spouse to create an incentive contract that provides rewards for specific behavioral changes. Learn to reward each other for meeting specified goals. By doing this work, you will provide encouragement, praise and behavioral reinforcement, thus making your marriage last forever.

Write your plan of action here:

_____

_____

_____

_____

_____

_____

_____

_____

_____

_____

_____

_____

_____

_____

_____

Marriage Sustainment Strategy #77

Avoid Making False Accusations

Make It Last Forever:

Never accuse your spouse of wrongdoing without evidence.

You at work:

Have evidence to back your accusation or claim. No one likes to be falsely accused. However, do not look for things to create drama in your marriage or speak falsely in any matter about your spouse. By doing this work, you will avoid and minimize deception, thus making your marriage last forever.

Write your plan of action here:

_____

_____

_____

_____

_____

_____

_____

_____

_____

_____

_____

_____

Marriage Sustainment Strategy #78

Be Adventurous

Make It Last Forever:

Be adventurous.

You at work:

Engage in a team-building activity that requires you and your spouse to depend on each other. Such an experience can enhance and/or restore trust. By doing this work, you will nurture the deep love you have for each other, thus making your marriage last forever.

Write your plan of action here:

_____

_____

_____

_____

_____

_____

_____

_____

_____

_____

_____

_____

_____

_____

_____

_____

Marriage Sustainment Strategy #79

Demonstrate Faith in Your Spouse

Make It Last Forever:

When things are not going well in your marriage or life in general, let your spouse know that you believe in him or her.

You at work:

Demonstrate faith in your spouse. Remember that faith is associated with the unknown. We do not always have the answers or solutions to our problems, but we feel more in control when others believe in and depend on us. Boost your spouse's confidence and promote a can-do attitude. By doing this work, you can help reduce your spouse's anxiety and fear of letting you down, thus making your marriage last forever.

Write your plan of action here:

_____
_____
_____
_____
_____
_____
_____
_____
_____
_____
_____

Marriage Sustainment Strategy #80

Make Your Spouse a Priority

Make It Last Forever:

Your spouse should be your number one priority and your attitude should never be one of indifference. It is okay and normal to be angry occasionally, but not to be indifferent.

You at work:

Never treat your spouse nonchalantly. Do not deny him or her the compassion and love that you have in your heart. By doing this work, you will reinforce your vows and bond, thus making your marriage last forever.

Write your plan of action here:

_____
_____
_____
_____
_____
_____
_____
_____
_____
_____
_____
_____
_____
_____
_____
_____

Marriage Sustainment Strategy #81

Document Your Appreciation

Make It Last Forever:

Expressing your appreciation can help prevent and minimize marital complacency.

You at work:

Write an appreciation letter to your spouse. After years of being in love, individuals have a tendency to take each other for granted and fail to express their gratitude. A simple "thank you" can go a long way, especially if your spouse is feeling unappreciated. By doing this work, you can provide your spouse with a tangible token that reflects what's in your heart, thus making your marriage last forever.

Write your plan of action here:

_____

_____

_____

_____

_____

_____

_____

_____

_____

_____

_____

_____

_____

Marriage Sustainment Strategy #82

Be a Professional Confidant

Make It Last Forever:

Be a professional confidant and demonstrate an interest in your spouse's work life. Look for opportunities to offer support that can help your spouse cope with occupational stressors in an effective manner.

You at work:

Call your spouse at work at least once a week to inquire about his or her day. The call should be short in nature, but supportive. You know your spouse better than any of his or her coworkers. Listen and offer helpful coping information. By doing this work, you can gain better insight into your spouse's stressors and be better equipped to offer work-related support, thus making your marriage last forever.

Write your plan of action here:

_____
_____
_____
_____
_____
_____
_____
_____
_____
_____
_____

Marriage Sustainment Strategy #83

Exhibit Compassion and Empathy

Make It Last Forever:

Compassion and empathy enables you to show mercy and remorse.

You at work:

Exhibit compassion and empathy toward your spouse by placing yourself in his or her shoes. This allows you to be empathic. Trying to understand how your spouse feels will enable you to connect with him or her more effectively than you would by merely focusing on his or her actions or words. By doing this work, you will be able to focus on and address your spouse's emotional distress, thus making your marriage last forever.

Write your plan of action here:

_____

_____

_____

_____

_____

_____

_____

_____

_____

_____

_____

Marriage Sustainment Strategy #84

Court Your Spouse

Make It Last Forever:

Courting your spouse and making a commitment to marriage was just the beginning. Spending time alone and revisiting the foundation in which your marriage was built on can be very beneficial.

You at work:

Plan a date that you both will enjoy. This can be something you did when you first started dating or something completely new. Agree not to discuss stressful issues and spend the entire date reminiscing about the good times. Discuss joyful events and explore ways to relive them. By doing this work, you will feel refreshed and young at heart, thus making your marriage last forever.

Write your plan of action here:

_____

_____

_____

_____

_____

_____

_____

_____

_____

_____

Marriage Sustainment Strategy #85

Romance Your Spouse

Make It Last Forever:

Feelings of love are highest when individuals feel romantic and are being pampered.

You at work:

Create feelings of excitement and mystery. Have a candlelit dinner and hot bath with your spouse as often as time permits. Romance is healthy for the soul and spirit. Make time to relax with your spouse and love on him or her. By doing this work, you will keep your spouse excited and removed from everyday life, thus making your marriage last forever.

Write your plan of action here:

_____

_____

_____

_____

_____

_____

_____

_____

_____

_____

_____

_____

_____

_____

Marriage Sustainment Strategy #86

Pray for Your Marriage

Make It Last Forever:

Prayer is needed in marriage because no man or woman is perfect.

You at work:

Engage in spiritual communion with God on a regular basis. Prayer demonstrates your faith in God and can provide hope for you and your marraige. By doing this work, you acknowledge that God is the keeper of all things and is capable of instilling hope where it is lost, thus making your marriage last forever.

Write your plan of action here:

_____
_____
_____
_____
_____
_____
_____
_____
_____
_____
_____
_____
_____
_____

Marriage Sustainment Strategy #87

Practice Paraphrasing

Make It Last Forever:

The quickest way to prevent misunderstandings and conflict is to practice paraphrasing. Be slow to respond to your spouse, especially if you do not have a thorough and accurate understanding.

You at work:

Ninety percent of misunderstandings and conflict occur because individuals do not take the time to repeat what they heard. Instead they respond based on assumptions. You should practice paraphrasing and active listening to prevent misunderstandings and to clarify what you heard before responding. For example, "I heard you say……..and it makes you feel….." By doing this work, you will gain a better understanding and your spouse will feel understood, thus making your marriage last forever.

Write your plan of action here:

_____
_____
_____
_____
_____
_____
_____
_____
_____

Marriage Sustainment Strategy #88

Do Not Rebut

Make It Last Forever:

Do not listen solely to rebut.

You at work:

Pay attention to what is being said to you instead of thinking about your response. Process what your spouse is saying before you develop your response. This will allow you to get the real meaning of your spouse's message. By doing this work, you will develop better listening skills, thus making your marriage last forever.

Write your plan of action here:

_____

_____

_____

_____

_____

_____

_____

_____

_____

_____

_____

_____

_____

_____

_____

Marriage Sustainment Strategy #89

Express Loving Words

Make It Last Forever:

Unfortunately, saying the words "I love you" often vanishes after years of marriage, but professing your love is needed in order to sustain admiration and affection.

You at work:

Make a conscious effort to tell your spouse that you love him or her regularly. There may be days that your spouse needs to hear those words more than other days, so attempt to say them daily and with sincerity. By doing this work, you will recreate a connection that is filled with fondness and love, thus making your marriage last forever.

Write your plan of action here:

_____
_____
_____
_____
_____
_____
_____
_____
_____
_____
_____
_____
_____

Marriage Sustainment Strategy #90

Be an Active Participant

Make It Last Forever:

Recognize that your participation is needed to make your marriage successful.

You at work:

Remain active in your marriage. No marriage can survive if one person is doing all the work. Give your time and attention to your spouse and marriage. By doing this work, you will prevent boredom and passivity from settling in, thus making your marriage last forever.

Write your plan of action here:

_____

_____

_____

_____

_____

_____

_____

_____

_____

_____

_____

_____

_____

_____

Marriage Sustainment Strategy #91

Live Harmoniously With Yourself

Make It Last Forever:

Harmony with your spouse begins with harmony within yourself.

You at work:

Eliminate internal power struggles. "You" versus "You" drama can cause marital discord. Learn to live harmoniously with yourself so that living with your spouse is possible. If you have unresolved personal issues, seek help and pray for healing. By doing this work, you will find personal harmony and balance, thus making your marriage last forever.

Write your plan of action here:

_____
_____
_____
_____
_____
_____
_____
_____
_____
_____
_____
_____
_____

Marriage Sustainment Strategy #92

Express Public Recognition

Make It Last Forever:

Praise your spouse publicly.

You at work:

Let family and friends know how wonderful your spouse is and talk big about his or her accomplishments publicly. By doing this work, your spouse will admire you and feel proud to be on your side, thus making your marriage last forever.

Write your plan of action here:

_____

_____

_____

_____

_____

_____

_____

_____

_____

_____

_____

_____

_____

_____

_____

_____

_____

_____

_____

Marriage Sustainment Strategy #93

Focus on the Here and Now

Make It Last Forever:

You cannot fix or resolve what happened in the past, but you can address what is currently happening.

You at work:

Bringing up old issues often complicates the issue(s) at hand, preventing conflict from getting resolved. Focus on one issue at a time and do not bring up old issues. By doing this work, you can create the change you would like to see in the future, thus making your marriage last forever.

Write your plan of action here:

_____
_____
_____
_____
_____
_____
_____
_____
_____
_____
_____
_____
_____
_____
_____

Marriage Sustainment Strategy #94

Realize That Little Things Do Matter

Make It Last Forever:

Bottled up frustration will manifest itself in some form or fashion.

You at work:

Sweat the small stuff before it snowballs. If you are bothered by something, please do not suppress it. Let your spouse know how you feel before you are consumed with resentment and anger. By doing this work, you are more likely to resolve issues before they become too overwhelming, thus making your marriage last forever.

Write your plan of action here:

_____

_____

_____

_____

_____

_____

_____

_____

_____

_____

_____

_____

Marriage Sustainment Strategy #95

Think Success

Make It Last Forever:

Have a victorious mindset and set your spouse and marriage up for success.

You at work:

Expect only the best from your spouse and allow him or her to choose goals that are of value to him or her and give the greatest satisfaction. Build up your spouse by focusing on and helping him or her capitalize on his or her God-given internal drives and strengths. By doing this work, you and your spouse will achieve your wildest dreams, thus making your marriage last forever.

Write your plan of action here:

_____
_____
_____
_____
_____
_____
_____
_____
_____
_____
_____
_____
_____

Marriage Sustainment Strategy #96

Do Not Label Your Spouse

Make It Last Forever:

Do not assign labels to your spouse. Labels, such as lazy, inflexible, incompetent, stupid, naïve and stubborn, cause individuals to become defensive, even if there is some truth in what is said.

You at work:

Simply describe the behavior without assigning a label to your spouse. Help them understand your concerns about their behavior without attaching negative labels. By doing this work, you can minimize defensive reactions and facilitate open dialogue, thus making your marriage last forever.

Write your plan of action here:

_____
_____
_____
_____
_____
_____
_____
_____
_____
_____

Marriage Sustainment Strategy #97

Eliminate Bad Habits

Make It Last Forever:

Bad habits are bad because they are damaging in nature. Make sure that your spouse is not negatively impacted by your habits.

You at work:

Eliminate and discontinue habits that cause harm to your marriage: gambling, excessive video game playing, partying, adult entertainment (strip clubs, porn movies, etc.), flirting, etc. By doing this work, you will demonstrate selflessness and respect for your spouse, thus making your marriage last forever.

Write your plan of action here:

_____

_____

_____

_____

_____

_____

_____

_____

_____

_____

_____

_____

_____

_____

Marriage Sustainment Strategy #98

Regulate Emotional Synergy

Make It Last Forever:

Emotions expressed in tense and unhealthy environments typically do not get resolved in a non-threatening or productive manner. There is a place and time for everything.

You at work:

Encourage your spouse to express emotions when it is healthy and appropriate to do so. Not during tense situations. Set the stage for healthy expression of emotions and coping. By doing this work, you will be better equipped to generate positive emotional synergy, thus making your marriage last forever.

Write your plan of action here:

_____
_____
_____
_____
_____
_____
_____
_____
_____
_____
_____
_____
_____

Marriage Sustainment Strategy #99

Become a Proverbs 3:6 Spouse

Make It Last Forever:

To make your marriage last forever, you have to work. The good news is that most of the hard work and sacrifice has been done for you.

You at work:

In all your ways, acknowledge Him, and He shall direct your path. Know that God is love and His Love conquers all. Put God first in your marriage. By doing this work, you will be able to accomplish the other 98 marriage sustainment strategies with little to no effort. Thank God!

Write your place of action here:

_____

_____

_____

_____

_____

_____

_____

_____

_____

_____

_____

_____

_____

_____

Conclusion

Making your marriage last forever should be your number one priority. You made a promise before God, family and friends to love your spouse until death do you part. In order to uphold your promise and make your marriage last forever, you have to fight for your marriage.

If you are not willing to fight for your marriage, you do not know how to select the right fights. Anything in life worth having is worth fighting for. Your marriage is worth fighting for. Do not waste your time fighting over petty things when you can use that energy to make your marriage last forever.

If you are not prepared to fight fairly and in a healthy manner, please get professional help. Marriage is not easy, but it is worth the fight. I pray to God that the love, trust and happiness that you desire be restored in your marriage. I also pray to God that you grow old with your spouse and separation comes only with death.

I am a believer in marriage and have learned that marriage is for anyone who is willing to give 100 percent. I did not say that you will be able to give 100 percent all the time. I said, "Be willing to give 100 percent."

You should be doing all, or at least most of these strategies to make your marriage last forever, not just one of them. One of these strategies can *help* your marriage last forever, however, but one alone cannot *make* it last forever.

If you apply all of the strategies outlined in this book, I can assure you that your marriage will endure through adversity and you will be on the fast road to everlasting love.

In my Keith Sweat voice, "Make it Last Forever."

Thanks for Taking the Journey with Me,

Dr. Dwayne L. Buckingham

For Coaching and Booking Information

99 Marriage Sustainment Strategies was inspired by thousands of couples from around the world who have experienced marital bliss and longevity in marriage by applying the strategies outlined in this book.

Dr. Buckingham is a highly acclaimed psychotherapist who has gained an outstanding reputation for helping couples save their marriages. Through his work in marital therapy, couples' seminars and speaking engagements, Dr. Buckingham has inspired thousands of individuals to give and get the very best in their marriage.

To schedule marriage coaching sessions or an event:

Email: RHCS@realhorizonsdlb.com or

R.E.A.L. Horizons Consulting Service
11431 Amherst Avenue #2665
Silver Spring, MD 20915

Attention: Booking Manager
(240) 242-4087

About the Author

Dwayne L. Buckingham, Ph.D., LCSW, BCD, is a psychotherapist and the Chief Executive Officer and Founder of R.E.A.L. Horizons Consulting Service, LLC in Silver Spring, Maryland. A commissioned officer in the United States Air Force for nearly a decade, he provided psychological assessments and treatment to over thirty thousand individuals, couples, groups, and families worldwide.

Dr. Buckingham currently serves as a commissioned officer in the United States Public Health Service and works at military medical treatment facility in Bethesda, Maryland. Dr. Buckingham is also an active member of the National Association of Social Workers and Kappa Alpha Psi Fraternity, Inc.

He is driven by the belief that every individual can improve his or her ability to cope with life challenges productively if given the opportunity and right support. Dr. Buckingham reminds individuals daily that a little understanding and education eliminates barriers and enables individuals to grow. Through coaching, consultation and training, he hopes to provide individuals with the knowledge and skills essential to establishing and maintaining a positive and productive lifestyle.

Dr. Buckingham conducts seminars for groups, families, organizations, and churches each year. Please visit his website at www.realhorizonsdlb.com for more information.

www.ingramcontent.com/pod-product-compliance
Lightning Source LLC
Chambersburg PA
CBHW030023290326
41934CB00005B/461